The Bible's Battlefields- Timeless Lessons from Ancient Wars

Joshua Rhoades

Published by Joshua Paul Rhoades, 2024.

THE BIBLE'S BATTLEFIELDS- TIMELESS LESSONS FROM ANCIENT WARS

First edition. August 22, 2024.

Copyright © 2024 Joshua Rhoades.

ISBN: 979-8227051875

Written by Joshua Rhoades.

Also by Joshua Rhoades

Courage Under Fire: David's Stand On The Battlefield
Jonah's Journey: Voices Of Redemption And Lessons In Obedience
The Furnace Of Faith: 12 Principles From The Heat Of Faith
Whispers of Hope: Inspiring Stories of Men's Prayers In Scripture
Frontier Legends: The Oregon Dream
Elijah: A Beacon Of Boldness
HOOK, LINE & SAVIOUR - Faith Reflections from Fishing
Driven By Faith: Motor Racing Inspired Christian Life
30 Day Devotional - Bold and Strong- Coffee Devotions for a Courageous Christian Walk
Authentic Christianity: The Heart of Old Time Religion
Consider The Ant - God's Tiny Preachers
Flee Fornication: The Plea For Purity
Renewed Hope- How to Find Encouragement in God
Sounding The Call - The Voice of Conviction
The Altar - Where Heaven Meets Earth
The Bible's Battlefields- Timeless Lessons from Ancient Wars
The Sacred Art of Silence - How Silence Speaks in Scripture
Under Fire- The Sanctity of the Traditional Biblical Home
Who Is on the Lord's Side? A Call to Righteousness

Introduction

In the pages of Scripture, we encounter the rich tapestry of human experience interwoven with divine intervention, a narrative where the battles fought long ago on dusty fields and within city walls carry profound significance for us today. The Bible's Battlefields: Timeless Lessons from Ancient Wars is not merely a recounting of historical conflicts but an exploration into the spiritual depths of these encounters, revealing lessons that are as relevant now as they were thousands of years ago. From the dawn of creation, the Bible portrays life as a series of confrontations between light and darkness, good and evil, faith and fear, obedience and rebellion. These are not just physical skirmishes over territory but spiritual battles that reflect the ongoing war within the human soul and between the forces of heaven and hell. As we delve into the accounts of these ancient wars, we are challenged to see beyond the swords, shields, and strategies, to perceive the underlying spiritual truths that God intended to teach His people through these dramatic events. Each battle recorded in the Bible is a microcosm of the larger spiritual battle that every believer faces—a battle for the heart, the mind, and the soul. These stories are not just about the past; they are about us, about the conflicts we face in our daily lives, and about the eternal struggle that every follower of Christ must engage in.

The Bible's battlefields are stages where the faith of God's people was tested, where their trust in His promises was put on the line, and where their obedience to His commands determined the outcome of their destinies. These battles reveal the nature of God—His power, His justice, His mercy, and His unwavering commitment to His covenant with His people. They also reveal the frailties and strengths of humanity—our fears, our doubts, our courage, and our capacity for faith. As we walk through these stories, from the Exodus and the conquest of Canaan to the defense of Jerusalem and beyond, we are invited to see ourselves in these ancient warriors, to learn from their successes and their failures, and to apply these timeless lessons to the spiritual battles we face today. The warfare we engage in may not involve swords and spears, but it is no less real. Our enemies are not flesh and blood, but spiritual forces of evil that seek to undermine our faith, distort our beliefs, and lead us away from the truth of God's Word. The Bible's battlefields offer us not just inspiration but practical strategies for engaging in this spiritual warfare—strategies that can lead us to victory in our own lives if we are willing to heed the lessons they teach.

One of the central themes we encounter in these biblical battles is the importance of obedience to God's Word. Time and again, the outcome of these battles was determined not by the strength of the armies or the brilliance of the strategies, but by the willingness of God's people to obey His commands. When Joshua led the Israelites against Jericho, it was not their military prowess that brought the walls down, but their obedience to God's seemingly illogical command to march around the city for seven days. This act of obedience, rooted in faith, unleashed the power of God and led to a miraculous victory. Similarly, when Gideon faced the overwhelming forces of the Midianites with just 300 men, it was his obedience to God's instruction to reduce his army that paved the way for victory. These stories remind us that God's ways are not our ways, and His thoughts are not our thoughts. He often calls us to act in ways that defy human logic, to trust in His wisdom even when it seems foolish to the world, and to obey His commands even when they seem difficult or impossible. The lesson here is clear: obedience to God is the key to victory in our spiritual battles. It is not enough to rely on our own understanding or to follow the wisdom of the world; we must trust in the Lord with all our hearts and lean not on our own understanding.

Faith is another crucial lesson that emerges from the Bible's battlefields. The victories won by God's people were not just the result of their obedience, but of their deep, unwavering faith in God's promises. David's defeat of Goliath is perhaps the most famous example of this. Armed with nothing but a sling and a few stones, David's victory over the giant was not a testament to his skill but to his faith in a God who was greater than any foe. David's confidence was not in his own abilities but in the power of God to deliver him from the hand of his enemy. This kind of faith—bold, audacious, and rooted in a deep trust in God's character and promises—is what enabled God's people to overcome impossible odds and secure victory. In our own lives, we are called to cultivate this same kind of faith, to believe that no matter how formidable our enemies may seem, no matter how insurmountable the obstacles in our path, God is able to give us the victory if we place our trust in Him. Faith is not just a feeling or a belief; it is an active, living trust in God that moves us to step out in obedience, even when the path ahead is uncertain.

Perseverance is another vital lesson we learn from the battles of the Bible. The conquest of the Promised Land was not achieved in a day, and many of the battles fought by God's people required persistence, endurance, and an unwavering commitment to the task at hand. The Israelites had to fight battle after battle to claim the land God had promised them, and each victory was a step closer to the fulfillment of that promise. This process required them to persevere through setbacks, to hold fast to God's promises even when the outcome was not immediately visible, and to keep moving forward in faith. The lesson of perseverance is especially relevant for us today, as we face challenges that do not resolve quickly or easily. Whether it is a personal struggle, a spiritual battle, or a challenge in our communities, we are called to persevere, to continue trusting in God's promises, and to keep fighting the good fight of faith. Perseverance is about more than just enduring hardship; it is about holding on to the hope that God will fulfill His promises in His perfect timing, and that the victory is already assured in Him.

The Bible's battlefields also teach us about the importance of preparation and readiness. Before going into battle, God's people were often instructed to prepare themselves, to consecrate themselves, and to make ready for the fight ahead. This preparation was both physical and spiritual. They were to arm themselves with the weapons of warfare, but more importantly, they were to arm themselves with the knowledge of God's Word, with prayer, and with a heart fully committed to His will. In the same way, we are called to prepare ourselves for the spiritual battles we will face. Ephesians 6 exhorts us to put on the full armor of God so that we can stand against the schemes of the devil. This armor—truth, righteousness, the gospel of peace, faith, salvation, and the Word of God—is our spiritual defense against the attacks of the enemy. But it is not enough to merely put on the armor; we must be vigilant, always ready to stand firm in the face of opposition, and always prepared to defend our faith. The battles of the Bible remind us that victory is not just about being strong; it is about being prepared, about being ready to stand firm in the faith, and about being equipped with the spiritual tools we need to overcome the challenges we face.

Unity is another powerful lesson we learn from the Bible's battlefields. Many of the battles fought by God's people required them to come together as one, to fight not as individuals but as a united body. When the Israelites faced the Amalekites, Moses stood on a hill with his hands raised in prayer, and as long as his hands were raised, the Israelites prevailed. But when his hands grew tired, Aaron and Hur came alongside him, holding up his hands until the battle was won. This story illustrates the power of unity and the importance of standing together in the face of adversity. In our own spiritual battles, we are not meant to fight alone. We are part of the body of Christ, and our strength comes from our unity with other believers. When we stand together, pray for one another, and support each other in our struggles, we are stronger and more resilient. The enemy seeks to divide and isolate us, knowing that we are weaker when we are alone. But when we stand united in faith, we are able to withstand the attacks of the enemy and secure the victory that God has promised us.

Perhaps the most significant lesson we learn from the Bible's battlefields is the understanding that the battle belongs to the Lord. Time and again, we see that the victories won by God's people were not the result of their own strength or ingenuity, but of God's intervention on their behalf. Whether it was the walls of Jericho falling at the sound of a trumpet, the sun standing still for Joshua, or an angel of the Lord defeating an entire army, the common thread is that God was the one who secured the victory. This teaches us that in our own battles, while we must do our part, we must also recognize that the ultimate victory is God's. It is His power, His wisdom, and His might that will bring us through to the other side. This realization brings both humility and confidence—humility in acknowledging our dependence on God, and confidence in knowing that with Him on our side, no enemy can stand against us.

As we embark on this journey through The Bible's Battlefields: Timeless Lessons from Ancient Wars, we are invited to see these stories not just as accounts of the past, but as living lessons for our lives today. The battles we face—whether they are personal struggles, spiritual conflicts, or challenges in our communities—are opportunities for us to apply these timeless lessons, to grow in our faith, and to experience the victory that God has already secured for us through Christ.

These stories challenge us to trust in God's promises, to obey His commands, to persevere in the face of difficulty, to prepare ourselves for the battles ahead, to stand united with other believers, and to recognize that the battle belongs to the Lord. As we apply these lessons to our own lives, we will find that we are not alone in our struggles, that God is with us, fighting for us, and that in Him, we have already won the victory. The battlefields of the Bible are not just places where wars were fought; they are places where faith was tested, where God's power was revealed, and where the eternal struggle between good and evil played out in the lives of real people. As we journey through these stories, may we be inspired to fight the good fight of faith, to stand firm in the face of adversity, and to walk in the victory that is ours through Jesus Christ. The lessons learned on these battlefields are not just for the warriors of old; they are for us, for every believer who seeks to live a life of faith, obedience, and victory in the face of life's challenges. Let us, therefore, take up the lessons of the Bible's battlefields, arm ourselves with the truth of God's Word, and step onto the battlefield of life with confidence, knowing that the battle belongs to the Lord and that in Him, we are more than conquerors.

Chapter 1 – The Battle of Destruction

The Battle of Jericho is one of the most famous stories in the Old Testament, found in the book of Joshua, chapter 6. It tells about how the Israelites, led by Joshua, captured the city of Jericho in a very unusual way. After wandering in the desert for 40 years, the Israelites were finally ready to enter the Promised Land. Jericho was the first city they needed to conquer. Jericho was a strong city with thick walls, making it seem impossible to defeat. But God had a special plan for Joshua and the Israelites. God gave Joshua specific instructions on how to take the city. He told Joshua to have his army march around the city once a day for six days. During this time, the soldiers were not to say a word; they just had to march silently. Seven priests carrying trumpets made from ram's horns walked ahead of the Ark of the Covenant, which was a special box that held the Ten Commandments and represented God's presence. The priests would blow the trumpets as they marched, but the soldiers were to remain silent. On the seventh day, things were different. God told Joshua to have the army march around the city seven times. After the seventh time, the priests were to blow their trumpets, and Joshua told the soldiers to shout as loud as they could. Joshua followed God's instructions exactly. For six days, the soldiers marched silently once around the city, with the priests blowing their trumpets and the Ark of the Covenant being carried behind them. The people of Jericho must have been very confused and maybe even a little scared seeing this unusual display. On the seventh day, the Israelites got up at dawn and began their march. They circled the city seven times just as God had commanded. After the seventh time, the priests blew their trumpets, and Joshua commanded the soldiers to shout. The soldiers shouted with all their might, and something miraculous happened: the thick walls of Jericho collapsed! The city was wide open for the Israelites to capture. They rushed in and took the city, just as God had promised. This victory was not because of the Israelites' military strength but because they trusted and obeyed God's unusual instructions. The lesson from the Battle of Jericho is about the power of obedience to God. Sometimes God's instructions may seem strange or difficult to understand, but He has a purpose and plan that we may not see. The Israelites' victory at Jericho shows that when we trust and obey God, even when it doesn't make sense, He can do amazing things. It teaches us that faith and obedience are key to overcoming the obstacles we face in life. Just like the Israelites, we might face situations that seem impossible to handle. But if we follow God's guidance and have faith in His power, we can see incredible results. The story of Jericho reminds us that God is always with us and that His ways are higher than our ways. It encourages us to listen to His voice, trust in His plans, and act in faith, knowing that He can bring down any walls that stand in our way. This story also shows that God keeps His promises. He had promised the Israelites the land of Canaan, and Jericho was the first step in fulfilling that promise. God's faithfulness to His word is evident, and it reassures us that we can trust Him to keep His promises to us as well. The fall of Jericho is not just a story of a military victory but a powerful example of what can happen when we put our trust in God and follow His lead, no matter how unconventional His instructions may seem.

Chapter 2 – The Battle of Deception

The Battle of Ai is a fascinating and instructive story found in Joshua chapters 7 and 8 in the Old Testament. It tells about how the Israelites, under Joshua's leadership, faced a surprising defeat due to sin within their camp and how they later turned that defeat into a decisive victory through repentance and strategic planning. After the Israelites' incredible victory at Jericho, they were confident and ready to conquer the next city, Ai. However, they did not know that one of their own, Achan, had disobeyed God's command during the Jericho campaign by taking some of the devoted things, which were supposed to be destroyed or given to God's treasury. Because of Achan's sin, God was not with the Israelites as they went to battle Ai. Joshua sent a small force of about three thousand men to attack Ai, thinking it would be an easy victory. However, the men of Ai fought fiercely, and the Israelites were soundly defeated, with about thirty-six of their men killed. This unexpected defeat caused great fear and confusion among the Israelites. Joshua and the elders of Israel tore their clothes, put dust on their heads, and fell face down before the Ark of the Covenant, praying and seeking God's guidance. God revealed to Joshua that Israel had sinned and broken the covenant by taking some of the devoted things. God instructed Joshua to consecrate the people and remove the sin from among them. The next day, Joshua gathered all the tribes of Israel, and through a process of elimination, Achan's sin was revealed. Achan confessed to taking a beautiful robe, two hundred shekels of silver, and a bar of gold, which he had hidden in the ground inside his tent. Achan, along with his family and possessions, was brought to the Valley of Achor, where they were stoned and burned as a punishment for his sin and as a way to remove the curse from Israel. With the sin addressed and the camp purified, God gave Joshua new instructions on how to conquer Ai. This time, Joshua devised a clever plan using deception and an ambush. He set an ambush behind the city and took a main force of soldiers to approach the city from the front. The plan was to pretend to retreat as they had done before, drawing the men of Ai out of the city. When the men of Ai chased after the retreating Israelites, the ambush force would enter the city and set it on fire. Joshua followed God's instructions and his plan perfectly. The main force approached Ai, and as expected, the men of Ai came out to attack them, leaving the city unprotected. The Israelites pretended to flee, and the men of Ai pursued them. At that moment, Joshua stretched out his javelin toward Ai, signaling the ambush force to rise and enter the city. They quickly took the city and set it on fire. The men of Ai, seeing their city burning, were thrown into confusion. The retreating Israelites turned back to fight, and the ambush force came out to attack from the other side. The men of Ai were trapped between the two forces and were completely defeated. This time, the Israelites achieved a decisive victory, and the city of Ai was captured and destroyed. The story of the Battle of Ai teaches several important lessons. First, it shows the serious consequences of sin and disobedience to God's commands. Achan's sin not only brought defeat to the Israelites but also caused the death of many people. This emphasizes the importance of personal and communal integrity and obedience to God. Second, it highlights the need for repentance and seeking God's guidance. When Joshua and the Israelites realized their mistake, they sought God's help, repented, and addressed the sin in their midst. This act of repentance restored their relationship with God and brought His favor back upon them. Third, the story demonstrates that with God's guidance, even a previous defeat can be turned into victory. By following God's new instructions and using strategic planning, Joshua was able to lead the Israelites to a successful conquest of Ai. This teaches us that failures and setbacks can be overcome when we align ourselves with God's will and seek His direction. In modern application, the Battle of Ai reminds us of the importance of living a life of integrity and obedience to God. When we face defeats or challenges, it is crucial to examine ourselves, repent of any wrongdoing, and seek God's guidance. Just as the Israelites turned their initial defeat into a victory through repentance and following God's plan, we too can overcome obstacles and achieve success when we trust in God's wisdom and direction. The story encourages us to remain faithful and obedient to God, knowing that He is always ready to help us turn our defeats into victories when we seek Him with a sincere heart.

Chapter 3 – The Battle of Defense

The Battle of Gibeon is an exciting and miraculous story found in Joshua chapter 10 in the Old Testament. It shows how the Israelites, led by Joshua, defended the Gibeonites against a powerful alliance of Amorite kings and how God intervened in a supernatural way to ensure their victory. The Gibeonites, who lived in the land of Canaan, had recently made a treaty with the Israelites, which was unusual because the other Canaanite cities were enemies of Israel. This treaty angered the surrounding Amorite kings, who decided to join forces and attack Gibeon for aligning with Israel. The five Amorite kings – those of Jerusalem, Hebron, Jarmuth, Lachish, and Eglon – gathered their armies and laid siege to Gibeon, hoping to punish them for their treaty with Israel and to discourage other cities from doing the same. The Gibeonites, realizing they were in great danger, sent an urgent message to Joshua at his camp in Gilgal, pleading for immediate help. They said, "Do not abandon your servants. Come up to us quickly and save us! Help us, because all the Amorite kings from the hill country have joined forces against us." Joshua, honoring the treaty and trusting in God's promises, responded swiftly. He gathered his best warriors and marched all night from Gilgal to Gibeon. Despite the exhausting march, Joshua's troops arrived in Gibeon by morning, ready to fight. God reassured Joshua, telling him, "Do not be afraid of them; I have given them into your hand. Not one of them will be able to withstand you." With this divine assurance, Joshua and his army launched a surprise attack on the Amorite coalition. The sudden appearance of the Israelites and the ferocity of their attack caused the Amorite armies to panic. As the battle raged, God provided even more direct assistance. He threw the Amorites into confusion, making it difficult for them to fight effectively. The Israelites pursued their enemies, striking them down as they fled. The Amorites ran towards the descent to Beth Horon and even further towards Azekah and Makkedah, but the Israelites were relentless in their pursuit. During the chase, God demonstrated His power in a spectacular way. He hurled large hailstones from the sky upon the fleeing Amorites. The hailstones were so deadly that more Amorites died from the hail than from the swords of the Israelites. This divine intervention showcased God's control over nature and His commitment to fighting for His people. Despite these miraculous events, the day was slipping away, and Joshua needed more time to completely defeat the Amorite armies. In an extraordinary act of faith, Joshua prayed to God in front of all the Israelites, asking for the sun to stand still over Gibeon and the moon over the Valley of Aijalon. God granted Joshua's request, and the sun stopped in the middle of the sky and delayed going down for about a full day. This unprecedented event allowed the Israelites to continue their pursuit and ensure a total victory. The extended daylight gave them the time they needed to crush their enemies completely. The Bible notes that there has never been a day like it before or since, a day when the Lord listened to a human being. This incredible miracle emphasized that God was fighting for Israel. The Israelites returned to their camp at Gilgal after the battle, victorious and in awe of the mighty acts of God they had witnessed. They had defended their allies, the Gibeonites, and defeated a formidable enemy coalition through faith, obedience, and divine intervention. The Battle of Gibeon teaches us several valuable lessons. First, it shows the importance of honoring commitments and alliances. Joshua and the Israelites upheld their treaty with the Gibeonites, even though it was politically inconvenient and dangerous. This act of integrity was blessed by God. Second, the story illustrates the power of trusting in God and seeking His guidance in times of adversity. Joshua and his army relied on God's promises and support, which led to their miraculous victory. God's intervention with the hailstones and the extended daylight demonstrated His willingness to fight for those who trust in Him. Third, the battle emphasizes the importance of bold faith. Joshua's prayer for the sun to stand still was a daring request, but it was rooted in his unwavering belief in God's power and willingness to assist His people. This act of faith resulted in one of the most remarkable miracles recorded in the Bible. For Christians today, the Battle of Gibeon is a powerful reminder that God is always with us and ready to support us when we face challenges. It encourages us to uphold our commitments, trust in God's power, and have faith that He will intervene on our behalf. Just as God fought for Israel, He fights for us when we call on Him and rely on His strength. The story reassures us that no matter how difficult or overwhelming our circumstances may be, God is capable of doing the impossible to bring about our deliverance and victory. We are reminded to seek God's guidance, act with integrity, and trust in His mighty power, knowing that He is faithful to those who place their faith in Him. The Battle of Gibeon stands as a testament to God's unfailing support and the incredible outcomes that can result from our trust and faith in Him.

Chapter 4 - Battle of Deliverance

The Battle of Mount Tabor, found in Judges chapters 4 and 5 in the Old Testament, is a dramatic and inspiring story about deliverance and how God raises leaders to free His people from oppression. The Israelites, having fallen into sin and idolatry, were suffering under the harsh rule of King Jabin of Canaan, whose military commander, Sisera, had a powerful army with 900 iron chariots. The Israelites were oppressed for twenty years and cried out to the Lord for help. During this time, Deborah, a prophetess and judge of Israel, was leading the people with wisdom and fairness. She held court under the Palm of Deborah, where the Israelites came to her to settle their disputes. One day, God spoke to Deborah, instructing her to summon Barak, the son of Abinoam, from Kedesh in Naphtali. God had a plan to deliver the Israelites from the Canaanite oppression, and Deborah was to relay this message to Barak. When Barak arrived, Deborah told him that the Lord commanded him to take ten thousand men from the tribes of Naphtali and Zebulun and lead them to Mount Tabor. God promised that He would lure Sisera, the commander of Jabin's army, to the Kishon River and give him into Barak's hands. Barak agreed to go, but he requested that Deborah accompany him. Deborah agreed, but she warned Barak that the honor of the victory would not go to him because the Lord would deliver Sisera into the hands of a woman. Barak and Deborah then summoned the ten thousand men, and they marched to Mount Tabor. When Sisera heard that Barak had gone up to Mount Tabor, he gathered all his nine hundred iron chariots and all his men and marched to the

Kishon River. Deborah encouraged Barak, saying, "Go! This is the day the Lord has given Sisera into your hands. Has not the Lord gone ahead of you?" With this assurance, Barak and his men charged down Mount Tabor and attacked Sisera's army. The Lord threw Sisera and his chariots and army into confusion before Barak, and Sisera's forces were routed. Barak pursued the chariots and army all the way to Harosheth Haggoyim, and all Sisera's troops fell by the sword; not a man was left. Sisera, however, fled on foot to the tent of Jael, the wife of Heber the Kenite, because there was an alliance between Jabin king of Hazor and the family of Heber the Kenite. Jael went out to meet Sisera and said to him, "Come, my lord, come right in. Don't be afraid." So he entered her tent, and she covered him with a blanket. Sisera, exhausted from the battle, asked for a drink of water. Instead, Jael gave him milk and covered him up. Standing at the entrance of the tent, Jael waited until Sisera had fallen into a deep sleep from exhaustion. Then she took a tent peg and a hammer and quietly approached him. With a swift and determined action, she drove the peg through his temple into the ground, and Sisera died. When Barak came by in pursuit of Sisera, Jael went out to meet him. "Come," she said, "I will show you the man you are looking for." So he went in with her, and there lay Sisera with the tent peg through his temple—dead. On that day, God subdued Jabin, the Canaanite king, before the Israelites. And the hand of the Israelites pressed harder and harder against Jabin king of Canaan until they destroyed him. The victory over Sisera and the Canaanite oppression was celebrated in a song of praise by Deborah and Barak, known as the Song of Deborah, found in Judges chapter 5. This song recounts the events of the battle, the bravery of the leaders and soldiers, and the divine intervention that led to their victory. It is a powerful reminder of God's faithfulness and His ability to deliver His people from their enemies. The Battle of Mount Tabor teaches several important lessons. Firstly, it shows that God raises leaders to bring deliverance. Deborah, a wise and courageous woman, was appointed by God to lead Israel during a time of great distress. Her leadership, along with Barak's military prowess, brought about the deliverance of the Israelites from Canaanite oppression. This reminds us that God can use anyone, regardless of gender or position, to fulfill His purposes and bring freedom to His people. Secondly, the story emphasizes the importance of trusting in God's appointed leaders and uniting under His direction. Barak's willingness to follow Deborah's guidance and the unity of the ten thousand men from Naphtali and Zebulun were crucial in achieving their victory. When God's people come together in faith and obedience, they can overcome even the most formidable enemies. Thirdly, the story highlights God's power and sovereignty in delivering His people. The confusion that fell upon Sisera's army, the courage of Jael, and the ultimate victory were all orchestrated by God. This teaches us that in times of adversity, we should rely on God's power and trust that He will fight for us and bring about our deliverance. Finally, the story of Jael shows that God can use unexpected people and means to achieve His purposes. Jael, a woman not even from Israel, played a pivotal role in the victory by killing Sisera. This reminds us that God's ways are higher than our ways, and He can work through anyone to bring about His plans. For Christians today, the Battle of Mount Tabor serves as a powerful reminder that God is our deliverer. It encourages us to trust in His appointed leaders, unite in faith, and rely on His power in times of trouble. Just as God delivered the Israelites from Canaanite oppression, He can deliver us from our struggles and challenges when we place our faith in Him. The story reassures us that God is always at work, raising leaders, and orchestrating events to bring about His purposes and deliverance for His people. By looking to God and following His guidance, we can experience the freedom and victory that He promises. The Battle of Mount Tabor is a testament to God's faithfulness, power, and the importance of trusting in Him and His appointed leaders for deliverance and victory over oppression.

Chapter 5 - Battle of the Diminished

The Battle of Gideon versus the Midianites, found in Judges 7, is an inspiring story of how God can achieve great things with small numbers and how trusting in God rather than relying on human strength or numbers brings true victory. The Israelites were being oppressed by the Midianites, who would invade their land, destroy their crops, and leave them with nothing. The people of Israel cried out to the Lord for help, and God chose Gideon to deliver them. Gideon was initially hesitant and doubted his ability to lead Israel, but God assured him that He would be with him. Gideon gathered an army of 32,000 men to fight the Midianites, but God had a different plan. God told Gideon that he had too many men because if they won with such a large army, the Israelites might boast that they saved themselves by their own strength. To demonstrate that victory comes from the Lord, God instructed Gideon to reduce the number of his soldiers. First, God told Gideon to announce that anyone who was afraid could leave and return home. Twenty-two thousand men left, leaving Gideon with ten thousand. But God said that there were still too many men. He then instructed Gideon to take the men down to the water to drink. God told Gideon to separate those who lapped the water with their tongues like a dog from those who kneeled down to drink. Three hundred men lapped the water with their hands to their mouths. God told Gideon that with these 300 men, He would save Israel and give the Midianites into their hands. The rest of the men were sent home. With only 300 men, Gideon was now ready to follow God's plan. Gideon divided his 300 men into three groups and gave each man a trumpet, an empty jar, and a torch inside the jar. They surrounded the Midianite camp at night. Gideon instructed his men to follow his lead. When Gideon blew his trumpet, all the men were to blow their trumpets, break the jars, and shout, "For the Lord and for Gideon!" At Gideon's signal, the 300 men blew their trumpets, broke the jars, and held the torches high, shouting their battle cry. The sudden noise and lights caused confusion and panic among the Midianites. The Lord caused the Midianites to turn on each other with their swords. The enemy army fled, and Gideon's men pursued them. Despite their small number, the 300 Israelites achieved a great victory over the Midianites. The story of Gideon and his 300 men teaches us several important lessons. First, it shows that God can achieve great things with small numbers. The victory over the Midianites was not because of the size of Gideon's army but because of God's power and guidance. This reminds us that God does not need large numbers or great strength to accomplish His purposes. He can use anyone, no matter how small or weak, to bring about His will. Second, the story emphasizes the importance of trusting in God rather than relying on human strength or numbers. Gideon trusted God's plan, even though it meant reducing his army to just 300 men. This trust and obedience led to a miraculous victory. It teaches us that our success does not depend on our resources or abilities but on our faith in God and our willingness to follow His guidance. Third, the story of Gideon shows that God's ways are often different from our ways. Gideon would never have thought to fight with such a small number of men, but God's plan was to demonstrate His power and ensure that the Israelites knew that their victory was from Him. This teaches us to be open to God's leading, even when it doesn't make sense to us. God's wisdom and power are far greater than ours, and He knows the best way to achieve His purposes. For Christians today, the Battle of Gideon versus the Midianites is a powerful reminder that God is with us and can use us for great things, no matter how small or inadequate we may feel. It encourages us to trust in God's power rather than our own strength and to follow His guidance, knowing that He can bring about victory in the most unlikely circumstances. The story reassures us that God is always in control and that our faith in Him is the key to overcoming challenges and achieving success. Gideon's victory with just 300 men stands as a testament to the power of faith, trust, and obedience to God. It reminds us that when we rely on God and follow His direction, we can accomplish great things for His glory. The story of Gideon and the Midianites encourages us to step out in faith, trust in God's plan, and believe that He can work through us to achieve His purposes, no matter how daunting the task may seem. This powerful story from Judges 7 teaches us that true victory comes from God, and when we place our trust in Him, we can overcome any obstacle and experience the deliverance and success that He has promised.

Chapter 6 – The Battle of the Duel

The Battle of David and Goliath, found in 1 Samuel 17, is one of the most well-known and inspirational stories in the Old Testament, showcasing the power of faith and courage in overcoming seemingly insurmountable challenges. The story begins with the Israelites and the Philistines preparing for battle in the Valley of Elah. The Philistines had a champion named Goliath, a giant over nine feet tall, who wore heavy armor and carried a massive spear. Every day for forty days, Goliath came forward and challenged the Israelites to send out a champion to fight him in single combat, but no one in Israel's army, including King Saul, had the courage to face him. Goliath's challenge caused great fear among the Israelites, and they were dismayed and terrified. Meanwhile, David, a young shepherd boy, was sent by his father Jesse to the battlefield to bring food to his older brothers who were fighting in Saul's army. When David arrived, he heard Goliath's challenge and saw the fear it instilled in the Israelites. David was surprised that no one had stepped up to fight the giant, and he was angered by Goliath's defiance of the armies of the living God. David, with unwavering faith in God, volunteered to fight Goliath. When King Saul heard about David's boldness, he initially dismissed David as just a boy, inexperienced in battle. However, David recounted how he had protected his father's sheep from lions and bears, trusting in God to deliver him from danger. David believed that the same God who had saved him from these predators would deliver him from Goliath. Saul, convinced by David's faith and determination, allowed him to face the giant. Saul offered David his own armor, but David found it cumbersome and decided to face Goliath with just his sling and five smooth stones he picked from a stream. Armed with his sling, stones, and his faith in God, David approached Goliath. Goliath looked down on David and mocked him, seeing only a young boy coming to fight with sticks. But David, full of confidence in God's power, replied, "You come against me with sword and spear and javelin, but I come against you in the name of the Lord Almighty, the God of the armies of Israel, whom you have defied. This day the Lord will deliver you into my hands, and I'll strike you down and cut off your head. This very day I will give the carcasses of the Philistine army to the birds and the wild animals, and the whole world will know that there is a God in Israel. All those gathered here will know that it is not by sword or spear that the Lord saves; for the battle is the Lord's, and he will give all of you into our hands." As Goliath moved closer to attack, David ran quickly toward the battle line to meet him. Reaching into his bag, David took out a stone, placed it in his sling, and hurled it at Goliath. The stone struck Goliath on the forehead, sinking into his skull, and Goliath fell facedown to the ground. David then ran over, stood over Goliath, took Goliath's sword, and used it to cut off the giant's head, sealing his victory. When the Philistines saw that their champion was dead, they turned and ran, and the men of Israel and Judah surged forward with a shout and pursued them, achieving a significant victory. The story of David and Goliath teaches several powerful lessons. First, it shows that faith in God empowers us to overcome our giants. David's victory was not due to his strength or military skill but because of his unwavering faith in God. He believed that God would deliver him, just as He had done before. This teaches us that no matter how big or daunting our challenges may seem, we can overcome them by placing our trust in God and relying on His power. Second, the story highlights the importance of facing challenges with confidence in God's power. David did not let fear or doubt deter him. Instead, he boldly confronted Goliath, knowing that God was with him. This reminds us that when we face difficulties, we should not be discouraged or afraid but should have confidence in God's ability to help us triumph. Third, David's refusal to wear Saul's armor teaches us the importance of being true to ourselves and using the gifts and tools God has given us. David knew that the armor was not right for him and chose to face Goliath with his sling, something he was skilled with and comfortable using. This teaches us to trust in the unique abilities and resources God has provided us rather than trying to be something we are not. For Christians today, the Battle of David and Goliath serves as a powerful reminder of the strength and courage that comes from faith in God. It encourages us to trust in God's power and to face our challenges with confidence, knowing that He is with us. The story reassures us that, no matter how intimidating our giants may be, we can overcome them through faith and reliance on God. David's victory over Goliath stands as a testament to the power of faith and the importance of trusting in God in the face of adversity. It inspires us to confront our fears and obstacles with the assurance that God will deliver us and bring about victory. The story of David and Goliath encourages us to be bold in our faith, to rely on God's strength, and to believe that with Him, we can conquer any giant that stands in our way. This timeless story from 1 Samuel 17 teaches us that true victory comes from God and that when we place our trust in Him, we can achieve great things and experience the triumph that He has promised.

Chapter 7 – The Battle of the Daring

The Battle of Michmash, recounted in 1 Samuel 14, is a story of daring and faith that led to an unexpected and decisive victory for Israel. This remarkable event centers around Jonathan, the son of King Saul, and his bold initiative to attack the Philistine garrison stationed at Michmash. At this time, the Israelites were in a precarious position, outnumbered and outgunned by the Philistines, who had superior weaponry and a vast army. The Philistines had established a stronghold at Michmash, creating a significant threat to the Israelites. King Saul and his troops were camped nearby in Gibeah, paralyzed by fear and uncertainty, unsure of how to confront the powerful Philistine force. In this tense situation, Jonathan decided to take matters into his own hands, demonstrating remarkable courage and faith. Without informing his father or the rest of the Israelite army, Jonathan and his armor-bearer secretly left the camp to approach the Philistine outpost. Jonathan believed that God could deliver Israel through just a few people if it was His will, showing his deep faith in God's power. He told his armor-bearer, "Come, let's go over to the outpost of those uncircumcised men. Perhaps the Lord will act in our behalf. Nothing can hinder the Lord from saving, whether by many or by few." His armor-bearer, sharing Jonathan's faith and bravery, replied, "Do all that you have in mind. Go ahead; I am with you heart and soul." Together, they devised a daring plan to reveal themselves to the Philistines. Jonathan proposed that if the Philistines invited them to come up to their position, it would be a sign that the Lord had given them into their hands. When Jonathan and his armor-bearer showed themselves to the Philistine garrison, the Philistines mocked them and invited them to climb up, saying, "Come up to us and we will teach you a lesson." Taking this as a sign from God, Jonathan and his armor-bearer climbed up the rocky cliff to reach the Philistine outpost. In a fierce and surprising attack, Jonathan and his armor-bearer struck down about twenty Philistines within a small area. This bold move caused panic and confusion among the Philistine troops, triggering a ripple effect throughout their camp. At the same time, God intervened by sending a trembling through the ground, further amplifying the chaos among the Philistines. The Philistines, in their confusion, turned on each other, and the Israelite forces, witnessing the commotion from a distance, took advantage of the opportunity to join the battle. Saul's lookouts in Gibeah saw the Philistine army melting away in all directions and reported this to Saul, who quickly mustered his troops. Realizing that Jonathan and his armor-bearer were missing, Saul called for the Ark of God, seeking divine guidance. However, the tumult in the Philistine camp grew so intense that Saul and his men joined the battle without waiting for further instructions. The Israelites rallied and pursued the fleeing Philistines, turning the tide of the battle in their favor. Even the Hebrew slaves who had been with the Philistines joined the Israelites, and those Israelites who had hidden in the surrounding hills came out to fight. The Lord delivered Israel that day, and the battle extended beyond Beth Aven as the Israelites chased the Philistines from their territory. The daring actions of Jonathan and his armor-bearer brought about a significant and unexpected victory for Israel, demonstrating the power of bold faith and initiative. This story teaches several important lessons. First, it highlights the impact of individual courage and faith. Jonathan's willingness to take a bold step, trusting in God's power, set off a chain reaction that led to a national victory. It shows that one person's faith and initiative can inspire others and lead to remarkable outcomes. Second, the story underscores the importance of relying on God rather than human strength or numbers. Jonathan's statement, "Nothing can hinder the Lord from saving, whether by many or by few," reflects his deep trust in God's ability to deliver His people regardless of the odds. This teaches us that faith in God is more important than the size of our resources or the strength of our forces. Third, the story of Michmash illustrates that God often works through unexpected and surprising means. The Israelites were not expecting such a victory, especially not one initiated by just two men. This reminds us that God can bring about success in ways we might not anticipate, using unlikely people and circumstances to achieve His purposes. For Christians today, the Battle of Michmash serves as an encouragement to act with bold faith and initiative. It challenges us to trust in God's power and step out in faith, even when the odds seem against us. Just as Jonathan's daring action led to a great victory, our courageous steps of faith can result in God's favor and success. The story reassures us that God is with us and can use our faith-filled actions to bring about His plans and purposes. The Battle of Michmash stands as a testament to the power of faith, courage, and reliance on God. It inspires us to be bold in our faith, to take initiative, and to trust that God can achieve great things through us, no matter how small or insignificant our efforts may seem. Jonathan's victory over the

Philistines reminds us that when we act in faith, trusting in God's power, we can experience unexpected and remarkable outcomes. The story encourages us to live boldly for God, knowing that He is able to do exceedingly abundantly above all that we ask or think, according to the power that works in us. The Battle of Michmash is a powerful example of how daring faith can lead to divine intervention and victory, and it calls us to trust in God and step out in faith in our own lives.

Chapter 8 The Battle of the Downfall

The Battle of Mount Gilboa, as detailed in 1 Samuel 31, is a significant and tragic story that marks the downfall of King Saul and his sons, leading to a profound defeat for Israel. The events leading up to this battle highlight the consequences of disobedience and straying from God's commands, and they serve as a somber reminder of the importance of faithfulness to God. The story unfolds during a turbulent period in Israel's history when the Philistines, a persistent enemy of the Israelites, posed a formidable threat. King Saul, who had been chosen as the first king of Israel, had long struggled with obedience to God's directives, often acting out of fear and insecurity rather than faith and trust in the Lord. This disobedience gradually led to his spiritual decline and alienation from God. As the Philistines gathered their forces to fight against Israel, they camped at Shunem, while Saul and the Israelite army set up their camp on Mount Gilboa. Saul, seeing the vast Philistine army, was terrified, and his heart was filled with dread. In his desperation, Saul sought guidance from the Lord, but God did not answer him, neither by dreams nor by prophets, as Saul had consistently disobeyed Him. In a final act of defiance and desperation, Saul sought out a medium to summon the spirit of the deceased prophet Samuel, despite having previously banned mediums and spiritists from the land in accordance with God's law. When Samuel's spirit appeared, he rebuked Saul, reminding him of his disobedience to God's commands, particularly regarding the Amalekites, and foretold that the Lord had torn the kingdom from Saul and given it to David. Samuel also predicted that Saul and his sons would perish in the upcoming battle, and Israel would fall into the hands of the Philistines. Despite this dire prophecy, Saul prepared for the battle. The next day, the Philistines attacked with full force, and the Israelites were quickly overwhelmed. The battle was fierce, and the Israelite army was in disarray. Many Israelites fled, and those who remained were slain. Saul's sons, Jonathan, Abinadab, and Malki-Shua, were killed in the fighting. As the battle pressed hard against Saul, he was critically wounded by the Philistine archers. Realizing that his end was near and not wanting to be captured and humiliated by the Philistines, Saul took his own sword and fell on it. His armor-bearer, seeing that Saul was dead, also fell on his sword and died with him. Thus, Saul, his three sons, his armor-bearer, and all his men died together that same day. The death of Saul and his sons marked a catastrophic defeat for Israel. When the Israelites on the other side of the valley and beyond the Jordan saw that the Israelite army had fled and that Saul and his sons were dead, they abandoned their towns and fled, allowing the Philistines to come and occupy them. The next day, the Philistines came to strip the dead and found Saul and his sons fallen on Mount Gilboa. They cut off Saul's head, stripped off his armor, and sent messengers throughout the land of the Philistines to proclaim the news in the temple of their idols and among their people. They put Saul's armor in the temple of the Ashtoreths and fastened his body to the wall of Beth Shan. When the people of Jabesh Gilead heard what the Philistines had done to Saul, all their valiant men marched through the night to Beth Shan. They took down the bodies of Saul and his sons from the wall of Beth Shan and went to Jabesh, where they burned them. Then they took their bones and buried them under a tamarisk tree at Jabesh, and they fasted seven days. The Battle of Mount Gilboa serves as a powerful lesson about the consequences of disobedience and departure from God. Saul's downfall was a direct result of his repeated failure to follow God's commands and his reliance on his own judgment rather than seeking and obeying God's will. His life and reign, which began with such promise, ended in tragedy and defeat because of his spiritual waywardness. This story underscores the crucial importance of remaining faithful to God's commands and the dangers of turning away from Him. Saul's tragic end illustrates that disobedience to God leads to downfall, not just for individuals but for the community they lead. The defeat at Mount Gilboa was not only a personal tragedy for Saul and his family but also a national disaster for Israel, resulting in significant loss of life, territory, and morale. For Christians today, the Battle of Mount Gilboa is a sobering reminder to heed God's instructions and remain faithful to His will. It teaches us that spiritual defeat and downfall often begin with small acts of disobedience and a gradual turning away from God. To avoid such a fate, we must cultivate a heart of obedience, seeking God's guidance in all things and trusting in His wisdom rather than our own understanding. The story also highlights the importance of godly leadership. Saul's failure as a leader had profound consequences for the nation of Israel. This serves as a reminder that those in positions of leadership bear a great responsibility to lead with integrity, humility, and a steadfast commitment to God's commands. The people they lead are profoundly affected by their actions and decisions. The Battle of Mount Gilboa also offers a glimmer of hope amidst the tragedy. The valor of the men of Jabesh Gilead in recovering and honoring the bodies of Saul and his sons demonstrates that even in the darkest times, acts of bravery and kindness can shine through. It shows that respect and honor for the fallen, and the willingness to do what is right, even at great personal risk, are values that endure. For believers, this story calls us to reflect on our own lives and the ways we may have strayed from God's path. It challenges us to repent of our disobedience, seek God's forgiveness, and recommit ourselves to following Him faithfully. By doing so, we can avoid the pitfalls that led to Saul's downfall and instead walk in the blessings and favor that come from a life lived in obedience to God. The Battle of Mount Gilboa is a powerful testament to the consequences of disobedience and the importance of staying true to God's commands. It serves as a cautionary tale and a call to faithfulness, urging us to learn from Saul's mistakes and strive to live lives that honor God and follow His will.

Chapter 9 – The Battle of Divine Guidance

The Battle of Baal-perazim, detailed in 2 Samuel 5, is a compelling story that demonstrates the importance of seeking divine guidance and the success that comes from consulting God in all decisions. This battle marks a significant moment in King David's reign, showcasing his reliance on God and the divine victory achieved over the Philistines through faith and obedience. After David was anointed king over Israel, the Philistines, long-time enemies of Israel, sought to challenge his rule. They mobilized their forces and spread out in the Valley of Rephaim, posing a significant threat to David and his newly united kingdom. Recognizing the gravity of the situation, David did not rely solely on his military experience or the strength of his army. Instead, he sought the guidance of the Lord. David inquired of God, asking, "Shall I go and attack the Philistines? Will you deliver them into my hands?" God responded affirmatively, instructing David to go ahead with the assurance that He would deliver the Philistines into his hands. With this divine direction, David led his troops against the Philistines and achieved a resounding victory. He defeated them at Baal-perazim, a name that means "Lord of the Breakthrough," because David declared, "As waters break out, the Lord has broken out against my enemies before me." This victory was not just a military success but a testament to the power of seeking and following God's guidance. David's decision to consult God before engaging in battle highlights his dependence on divine wisdom rather than human strategy. This act of faith and obedience set the stage for a series of divinely orchestrated victories that characterized David's reign. However, the story did not end with this initial victory. The Philistines regrouped and once again spread out in the Valley of Rephaim. Faced with this recurring threat, David did not assume that the same strategy would work again. Instead, he sought God's guidance anew. This time, God gave David different instructions. He told David not to go straight up but to circle around behind the Philistines and attack them in front of the poplar trees. God instructed David to wait for the sound of marching in the tops of the trees, which would signal that the Lord had gone out ahead of him to strike down the Philistine army. David obeyed these specific instructions, and as soon as he heard the sound of marching in the tops of the trees, he launched his attack. The Philistines were once again defeated, and David's fame spread throughout the land as the Lord continued to grant him victory. The Battle of Baal-perazim teaches several vital lessons. First, it underscores the importance of seeking God's guidance in all decisions. David's consistent practice of inquiring of the Lord before making strategic moves ensured that he was aligned with God's will and direction. This reliance on divine guidance brought about successful outcomes and established David as a leader who prioritized God's wisdom over his own understanding. Second, the story illustrates that God's strategies may change, and being attuned to His voice is crucial. David did not rely on past experiences or victories but sought fresh guidance for each new challenge. This teaches us that while past successes are valuable, it is essential to seek God's current direction for new situations. God's guidance is specific to the circumstances we face, and His plans are perfect. Third, the story of Baal-perazim highlights the power of obedience to God's instructions. David's willingness to follow God's unconventional strategies, such as waiting for the sound of marching in the tops of the trees, demonstrated his trust in God's timing and methods. This obedience resulted in decisive victories and the establishment of David's kingdom. For Christians today, the Battle of Baal-perazim serves as a powerful reminder to seek God's guidance in every aspect of life. Whether facing personal challenges, making significant decisions, or leading others, consulting God ensures that our actions are aligned with His will. This story encourages us to develop a habit of prayer and seeking divine direction, trusting that God's wisdom surpasses our own and leads to successful outcomes. Moreover, the story teaches us to remain flexible and open to God's changing strategies. Just as David sought new guidance for each encounter with the Philistines, we must be willing to seek God's direction for each new situation we face. This ongoing dependence on God keeps us attuned to His will and ensures that we do not rely solely on past experiences or our own understanding. The Battle of Baal-perazim also highlights the importance of obedience to God's instructions. David's success was not just because he sought God's guidance but also because he faithfully followed the instructions given to him. This teaches us that seeking God's guidance must be accompanied by a willingness to obey His commands, even when they seem unconventional or challenging. Obedience to God's will leads to divinely orchestrated victories and establishes a foundation for lasting success. For leaders, this story emphasizes the significance of leading with dependence on God. David's example of seeking divine guidance and obeying God's instructions set a standard for godly leadership. Leaders who prioritize God's wisdom and direction can inspire confidence, unity, and success within their communities or organizations. The Battle of Baal-perazim, therefore, stands as a testament to the power of divine guidance and the importance of seeking and obeying God in all aspects of life. It reminds us that true success and victory come from aligning our actions with God's will and trusting in His perfect wisdom. This story encourages us to cultivate a lifestyle of seeking God's guidance through prayer and obedience, knowing that He will lead us to victory in every battle we face. In conclusion, the Battle of Baal-perazim is a profound story that teaches us the vital importance of seeking God's guidance and obeying His instructions. David's reliance on divine wisdom and his obedience to God's unconventional strategies resulted in significant victories over the Philistines and the establishment of his kingdom. For Christians today, this story serves as a powerful reminder to consult God in all decisions, remain flexible to His changing strategies, and faithfully obey His commands. By doing so, we can experience divinely orchestrated victories and achieve true success in our lives. The Battle of Baal-perazim stands as a testament to the power of divine guidance and the importance of living a life aligned with God's will.

Chapter 10 – The Battle of Disaster

The Battle of Absalom's Revolt, recounted in 2 Samuel 18, is a powerful story of rebellion, disaster, and the consequences of opposing God's anointed leader. This significant event in the history of Israel highlights the dangers of ambition and disobedience, while also underscoring the importance of respecting and supporting God's chosen leaders to ensure harmony and blessing. Absalom, the third son of King David, was a handsome and charismatic man who harbored deep-seated resentment towards his father for failing to bring justice to the rape of his sister Tamar by their half-brother Amnon. Over time, Absalom's bitterness grew, and he began to secretly plot to overthrow David and take the throne for himself. Absalom cunningly won the hearts of the people of Israel by presenting himself as a more accessible and caring leader than his father. He positioned himself at the city gate and intercepted those who came to seek the king's judgment, offering them sympathy and justice, and subtly criticizing David's administration. Over four years, Absalom's influence grew, and he gained the support of many, including some of David's trusted advisors, like Ahithophel. When the time was ripe, Absalom declared himself king in Hebron, a significant city in Judah, and sounded the trumpet to signal the start of his revolt. David, upon hearing of Absalom's treachery, was deeply troubled but chose to flee Jerusalem to avoid a bloody conflict within the city. Accompanied by his loyal followers, David crossed the Kidron Valley and ascended the Mount of Olives, weeping as he went. As David and his supporters fled, Absalom and his forces moved into Jerusalem, consolidating their power. David, although in exile, began to strategize on how to counter Absalom's rebellion. He sent his friend Hushai back to Jerusalem to act as a spy and to counter the advice of Ahithophel. Hushai, pretending to be loyal to Absalom, managed to convince him to delay an immediate attack on David's forces, giving David crucial time to regroup and prepare for battle. The stage was set for a decisive confrontation between the forces of Absalom and those loyal to David. David's army, commanded by experienced generals Joab, Abishai, and Ittai the Gittite, was divided into three groups. David, eager to join the battle himself, was persuaded by his men to remain behind in Mahanaim for his safety and to direct the battle from a secure position. The battle took place in the forest of Ephraim, a terrain that favored David's smaller but more experienced forces. The fighting was fierce and chaotic, with the dense forest claiming many lives, as the Bible notes that "the forest devoured more people that day than the sword." David's forces gained the upper hand, and Absalom's army was routed. In the midst of the battle, Absalom, riding on a mule, encountered some of David's men. As he fled, his long hair got caught in the branches of a large oak tree, leaving him hanging helplessly. One of David's soldiers saw Absalom and reported it to Joab, who, despite David's explicit orders to deal gently with his son, took three javelins and thrust them into Absalom's heart. Absalom's death marked the end of the rebellion and the defeat of his forces. Joab's men took down Absalom's body, cast it into a large pit in the forest, and piled a great heap of stones over it, a symbolic gesture of disgrace. The news of Absalom's death and the victory of David's forces was carried back to David by two messengers, Ahimaaz and a Cushite. David, anxiously awaiting word of the battle's outcome, was initially overjoyed to hear of the victory but was devastated when he learned of Absalom's death. He retreated to his chamber, weeping and lamenting, "O my son Absalom! My son, my son Absalom! If only I had died instead of you—O Absalom, my son, my son!" David's grief was profound and heartfelt, reflecting the deep love he had for his son despite Absalom's betrayal. The aftermath of the battle saw David returning to Jerusalem to reclaim his throne, but the kingdom had been deeply scarred by the rebellion. The lessons from Absalom's revolt are manifold. Firstly, the story vividly illustrates that rebellion against God's anointed leader leads to disaster. Absalom's ambition and his attempt to usurp the throne ended not only in his own death but also in the loss of many lives and the destabilization of the nation. This serves as a stark warning against the dangers of pride, ambition, and the desire for power. It underscores the importance of respecting and supporting those whom God has appointed to lead, recognizing that rebellion and disobedience bring only harm and destruction. Secondly, the story highlights the importance of justice and the consequences of failing to address wrongs. David's initial failure to properly deal with Amnon's crime against Tamar created a rift in his family and sowed the seeds of Absalom's rebellion. This teaches us that justice must be upheld, and grievances addressed to maintain harmony and prevent the growth of bitterness and resentment. Thirdly, the narrative showcases the complexities of leadership and the burden of decision-making. David's decision to flee Jerusalem and his strategic planning during the rebellion demonstrate his wisdom and experience as a leader. However, his deep sorrow over Absalom's death also reveals the personal pain and heartache that often accompany leadership. For Christians today, the story of Absalom's revolt is a reminder to trust in God's sovereignty and to support the leaders He has placed over us. It encourages us to cultivate a spirit of humility and obedience, recognizing that rebellion against God's appointed leaders is ultimately a rebellion against God Himself. The story also calls us to address wrongs and injustices in our lives and communities, understanding that unresolved issues can lead to greater conflict and division. Additionally, the story of Absalom's revolt invites us to reflect on the nature of true leadership. David, despite his flaws and mistakes, remained a man after God's own heart because he sought to follow God's will and lead his people with integrity. His grief over Absalom's death shows the compassionate and forgiving heart that made him a beloved leader. This teaches us that true leadership is characterized by humility, compassion, and a deep dependence on God. In conclusion, the Battle of Absalom's Revolt is a powerful story of disaster brought about by rebellion, and it serves as a cautionary tale about the importance of respecting and supporting God's anointed leaders. It highlights the destructive consequences of ambition and disobedience while also showcasing the complexities and burdens of leadership. For believers, it is a reminder to trust in God's sovereignty, seek justice, and cultivate a spirit of humility and obedience. The story of Absalom's revolt teaches us that true victory and harmony come from aligning ourselves with God's will and supporting those He has chosen to lead us.

Chapter 11 – The Battle of Desperation

The Battle of Ziklag, found in 1 Samuel 30, is a compelling and inspiring story that illustrates the power of seeking God's guidance in times of desperation, ultimately leading to the recovery of all that was lost and a renewed sense of hope and restoration. The narrative begins with David and his men returning to their home in Ziklag, a city given to David by the Philistine king Achish, where they had been living for some time. Upon their arrival, they found the city burned to the ground and their families taken captive by the Amalekites. This devastating sight filled David and his men with intense grief and despair. The loss of their loved ones and their homes left them in a state of utter desperation. David's men, already distressed and weary from their journey, were overwhelmed with sorrow and anger. In their anguish, they spoke of stoning David, blaming him for their misfortune. This was a moment of profound crisis for David, as he faced not only his personal grief but also the threat of mutiny from his own followers. In this moment of desperation, David turned to God for strength and guidance. Rather than succumbing to fear and hopelessness, David sought the Lord's help. He called for the priest Abiathar and asked him to bring the ephod, a sacred garment used for seeking God's will. David inquired of the Lord, asking, "Shall I pursue this raiding party? Will I overtake them?" God responded to David with a clear and encouraging answer: "Pursue them. You will certainly overtake them and succeed in the rescue." Empowered by this divine guidance, David set out with his six hundred men to pursue the Amalekites. However, two hundred of his men were too exhausted to continue and stayed behind at the Besor Valley, while the remaining four hundred pressed on. As they pursued, they encountered an Egyptian servant who had been abandoned by his Amalekite master. The Egyptian was weak and near death, but David's men gave him food and water, reviving him. In gratitude, the servant agreed to lead David to the Amalekite raiders, on the condition that David would not kill him or return him to his master. The servant guided David and his men to the Amalekite camp, where they found the raiders spread out across the land, celebrating their plunder from Ziklag and other regions. David and his men launched a surprise attack at dawn, catching the Amalekites off guard. The battle raged from twilight until the evening of the next day, and David's forces were victorious. They killed all the Amalekites except for four hundred young men who fled on camels. David recovered everything the Amalekites had taken, including his two wives, Ahinoam and Abigail, and all the women and children. Nothing was missing; everything that had been taken was restored. David also took a great amount of plunder from the Amalekites' camp. When David and his men returned to the Besor Valley, where the two hundred men had stayed behind, some of the men who had fought in the battle did not want to share the plunder with those who had not. They argued that those who did not fight should only receive their families back and nothing more. However, David, demonstrating his leadership and sense of justice, declared that everyone would share alike. He said, "No, my brothers, you must not do that with what the Lord has given us. He has protected us and delivered into our hands the raiding party that came against us. Who will listen to what you say?

The share of the man who stayed with the supplies is to be the same as that of him who went down to the battle. All will share alike." David made this a statute and ordinance for Israel from that day forward. This decision reinforced the unity and fairness among his followers and showed his recognition that the victory and plunder were blessings from God. The story of the Battle of Ziklag offers several profound lessons. First and foremost, it teaches us the importance of seeking God's guidance in times of desperation. David's immediate turn to God for help in his darkest hour is a powerful example of faith and reliance on divine direction. Instead of allowing despair to paralyze him, David sought God's will, which led to clear instructions and the promise of success. This act of faith in a moment of crisis brought about restoration and renewed hope. Secondly, the narrative underscores the power of God's promises. When David sought God's guidance, he received a promise of victory and recovery. This divine assurance gave David the strength and determination to pursue the Amalekites and reclaim what was lost. The fulfillment of God's promise in this story illustrates that God's word is trustworthy and that He is faithful to deliver on His promises, even in the most desperate circumstances. Thirdly, the story highlights the importance of compassion and justice. David's treatment of the Egyptian servant shows his compassion and willingness to help those in need, even when he himself was in a desperate situation. This act of kindness led to crucial information that enabled David to find and defeat the Amalekites. Additionally, David's fair distribution of the plunder demonstrates his commitment to justice and equality. By ensuring that all his men, regardless of their role in the battle, received an equal share, David fostered a sense of unity and fairness among his followers. For Christians today, the Battle of Ziklag serves as a powerful reminder of the importance of seeking God's guidance in times of crisis. It encourages us to turn to God in prayer when we face desperate situations, trusting that He will provide the wisdom and direction we need. The story reassures us that no matter how dire our circumstances may seem, God is capable of bringing about restoration and recovery when we rely on Him. The narrative also calls us to have faith in God's promises, knowing that He is faithful and His word is true. Even when we are faced with overwhelming challenges, we can hold onto God's promises and trust that He will fulfill them in His perfect timing. This trust in God's faithfulness can give us the strength and courage to persevere through difficult times. Furthermore, the story of Ziklag teaches us the value of compassion and justice. In our interactions with others, especially in times of crisis, showing kindness and fairness can lead to positive outcomes and foster unity within our communities. David's example of helping the Egyptian servant and ensuring fair treatment for all his men is a model for us to follow in our relationships and leadership roles. In conclusion, the Battle of Ziklag is a powerful story of desperation, faith, and divine guidance. It illustrates how seeking God's direction in times of crisis can lead to restoration and renewed hope. David's reliance on God, his compassion for others, and his commitment to justice serve as valuable lessons for believers today. By turning to God in our moments of desperation, trusting in His promises, and treating others with kindness and fairness, we can experience the same restoration and victory that David and his men achieved at Ziklag. This story encourages us to maintain our faith and reliance on God, knowing that He is always with us, ready to guide us through our darkest hours and lead us to recovery and renewal. The Battle of Ziklag stands as a testament to the power of divine guidance and the transformative impact of faith in times of desperation.

Chapter 12 – The Battle of Disregard

The Battle of Ramoth-Gilead, detailed in 1 Kings 22, serves as a dramatic and cautionary tale about the dire consequences of disregarding God's warnings. This significant battle involved King Ahab of Israel and King Jehoshaphat of Judah, and it ultimately led to Ahab's death and a significant defeat for Israel. The narrative begins with Ahab, the king of Israel, seeking to reclaim the city of Ramoth-Gilead from the Arameans. To bolster his forces, Ahab invited Jehoshaphat, the king of Judah, to join him in the campaign. Jehoshaphat agreed to support Ahab but insisted on seeking the Lord's guidance before proceeding. This insistence reflected Jehoshaphat's faith and respect for God's counsel. Ahab gathered around four hundred prophets, who unanimously assured him of victory, saying, "Go, for the Lord will give it into the king's hand." However, Jehoshaphat sensed something amiss and asked if there was another prophet of the Lord they could consult. Reluctantly, Ahab mentioned Micaiah, son of Imlah, but expressed his disdain for Micaiah, stating that Micaiah never prophesied anything good about him, only bad. Nevertheless, Micaiah was summoned, and initially, he mockingly echoed the other prophets' assurances of success. When pressed for the truth, Micaiah revealed a vision of Israel scattered on the hills like sheep without a shepherd, indicating Ahab's death. He also described a heavenly scene where a lying spirit had been permitted by the Lord to entice Ahab into going to battle so he would meet his doom. Ahab, furious at Micaiah's prophecy, ordered him to be imprisoned and fed only bread and water until he returned safely. Micaiah's final words were a chilling warning: "If you ever return safely, the Lord has not spoken through me." Despite this clear and dire warning, Ahab chose to disregard Micaiah's prophecy and proceeded with his plan to attack Ramoth-Gilead. Jehoshaphat, although uneasy, joined Ahab in the battle. To avoid being a target, Ahab decided to disguise himself, while urging Jehoshaphat to wear his royal robes. The Aramean king had instructed his chariot commanders to focus solely on killing the king of Israel. Seeing Jehoshaphat in his royal attire, the Aramean soldiers initially targeted him, but upon realizing he was not Ahab, they ceased their pursuit. Meanwhile, an Aramean soldier randomly shot an arrow that struck Ahab between the sections of his armor. Gravely wounded, Ahab instructed his chariot driver to retreat from the battle. Ahab propped himself up in his chariot, facing the Arameans until evening, and as the blood from his wound flowed to the floor of the chariot, he died. At sunset, a cry spread through the ranks: "Every man to his town. Every man to his land!" Israel's forces retreated in disarray, and Ahab's body was taken to Samaria for burial. The prophecy of Micaiah had been fulfilled; Ahab's disregard for God's warning had led to his death and Israel's defeat. The story of the Battle of Ramoth-Gilead teaches several crucial lessons. First and foremost, it highlights the consequences of ignoring God's warnings. Ahab's decision to disregard Micaiah's prophecy, despite its clear and dire nature, led directly to his downfall. This narrative underscores the importance of heeding God's counsel, as provided through His Word and His prophets. Ignoring divine warnings can lead to disastrous outcomes, as seen in Ahab's tragic end. The story also emphasizes the role of true prophets in conveying God's messages, even when they are unwelcome or difficult to hear. Micaiah's courage to speak the truth in the face of Ahab's hostility exemplifies the integrity and faithfulness required of God's messengers. It serves as a reminder that God's truth must be respected and heeded, regardless of how unpalatable it might be to those in power. Additionally, the story illustrates the danger of seeking counsel that merely affirms one's desires rather than seeking the genuine will of God. Ahab surrounded himself with prophets who told him what he wanted to hear, leading him to false confidence and ultimately to his demise. This teaches us to seek God's true guidance earnestly and to be wary of advice that simply conforms to our own wishes. For Christians today, the Battle of Ramoth-Gilead serves as a powerful reminder of the necessity of seeking and obeying God's guidance. It calls us to prioritize divine wisdom over human inclinations and to listen to God's warnings with humility and reverence. The narrative encourages believers to consult God earnestly in all decisions, understanding that His guidance is crucial for avoiding disaster and achieving true success. The story also underscores the importance of spiritual discernment. Jehoshaphat's insistence on seeking another prophet reflects a discerning heart that recognizes the need for genuine divine counsel. Believers are encouraged to develop such discernment, ensuring that the guidance they follow aligns with God's truth and not merely with comforting or convenient messages. Furthermore, the story highlights the importance of integrity and courage in delivering God's messages. Micaiah's willingness to speak the truth, despite knowing it would bring him harm, exemplifies the commitment required of God's messengers. This teaches believers to stand firm in their faith and to speak God's truth boldly, regardless of the consequences. The Battle of Ramoth-Gilead also serves as a cautionary tale for leaders. Ahab's failure to heed prophetic warnings led to his death and his nation's defeat, demonstrating the far-reaching impact of a leader's decisions. Leaders are reminded of their responsibility to seek and follow God's guidance, understanding that their choices affect not only themselves but also those they lead. In conclusion, the Battle of Ramoth-Gilead is a profound and cautionary tale about the dangers of disregarding God's warnings. Ahab's decision to ignore Micaiah's prophecy led to his death and Israel's defeat, underscoring the critical importance of heeding divine counsel. The story teaches believers to seek God's guidance earnestly, to develop spiritual discernment, and to prioritize divine wisdom over human inclinations. It also highlights the courage and integrity required of those who deliver God's messages and serves as a reminder to leaders of the profound impact of their decisions. The Battle of Ramoth-Gilead stands as a testament to the vital importance of respecting and obeying God's warnings, illustrating that true success and safety lie in adherence to His guidance.

Conclusion

As we conclude *The Bible's Battlefields: Timeless Lessons from Ancient Wars*, we stand at the crossroads of reflection and action, where the ancient stories of warfare in Scripture intersect with the daily struggles and spiritual battles of our modern lives. The narratives of Joshua at Jericho, David against Goliath, Gideon with his 300 men, and so many other biblical warriors serve not just as historical accounts but as divine blueprints for victory in the battles we face today. These stories are more than mere tales of conquest; they are living lessons that call us to examine our faith, our strategies, and our reliance on God. In these accounts, we see that true victory is never about the strength of the army or the size of the challenge, but about the depth of our trust in God, the obedience to His commands, and the perseverance in the face of overwhelming odds. The battlefields of the Bible teach us that God's ways are often unconventional and counterintuitive, yet they are always perfect, leading to outcomes that glorify Him and demonstrate His power. As we apply these lessons to our lives, we are challenged to approach our own battles with the same faith and courage that defined the heroes of Scripture. Whether we are facing personal struggles, spiritual warfare, or external challenges, we are called to trust in the God who never fails, to obey His Word even when it defies human logic, and to persevere in faith, knowing that victory belongs to the Lord. These ancient battles reveal that the key to victory is not in our abilities or resources, but in our alignment with God's will and our willingness to follow His lead, no matter how daunting the path may seem.

As we move forward from these lessons, the challenge is not simply to remember them but to integrate them into every aspect of our Christian walk. The battlefields of the Bible are not just relics of the past; they are mirrors reflecting the ongoing spiritual warfare we face as believers. The apostle Paul reminds us in Ephesians 6 that we do not wrestle against flesh and blood, but against principalities, powers, and spiritual forces of evil in the heavenly realms. This spiritual battle is continuous, and the lessons from the Bible's battlefields equip us to fight it effectively. To continue in the walk of a Christian means to daily arm ourselves with the truth of God's Word, just as the ancient warriors armed themselves for physical battle. The armor of God—truth, righteousness, peace, faith, salvation, and the Word of God—is not just a metaphor; it is our essential defense against the attacks of the enemy. As we don this armor, we are reminded of the importance of each piece, not just as individual virtues, but as part of a complete strategy for spiritual warfare. Truth guards us against the deceptions of the enemy, righteousness shields us from the accusations of sin, peace steadies our hearts amidst turmoil, faith extinguishes the fiery darts of doubt, salvation protects our minds from despair, and the Word of God serves as our offensive weapon, cutting through the lies and bringing light to the darkest situations. To walk in victory, we must be diligent in maintaining this armor, not just in moments of crisis, but in our everyday lives, cultivating a disciplined, prayerful, and obedient lifestyle that keeps us connected to God's power and guidance.

Furthermore, continuing in the lessons learned from these biblical battles means recognizing that we are part of a larger spiritual community. Just as the Israelites fought together under the leadership of Joshua or as Gideon's 300 men stood united in their mission, we too are called to fight not as isolated individuals but as members of the body of Christ. The strength of our community, our church, and our fellowship with other believers is crucial to our ability to withstand the attacks of the enemy and to achieve victory in our battles. We must therefore commit to supporting one another, bearing each other's burdens, and standing together in faith, knowing that our collective strength is greater than the sum of our individual parts. This sense of community also extends to our mission in the world.

Just as the battles of the Bible were often fought to secure the future of God's people, so too are our spiritual battles connected to the advancement of God's kingdom on earth. Every victory we achieve in our personal lives has the potential to impact others, to bring them closer to Christ, and to demonstrate the power of God's love and truth in a world that desperately needs it. To continue in these lessons is to recognize that our battles are not just about us, but about the greater mission of spreading the gospel, living out our faith with integrity, and being a light in the darkness.

Moreover, as we continue in the Christian walk, the lessons from the Bible's battlefields challenge us to develop a mindset of perseverance and resilience. The heroes of Scripture were not immune to fear, doubt, or discouragement, yet they chose to press on, trusting in God's faithfulness and power. In our own lives, we will undoubtedly face times of trial and adversity, moments when the battle seems overwhelming and the path to victory unclear. In these moments, we must remember the example of biblical warriors who stood firm in their faith, even when the odds were against them. Their stories remind us that God's timing is perfect, that He is with us in the midst of the battle, and that victory often comes after a period of waiting, testing, and endurance. To continue in this lesson is to cultivate a faith that does not waver in the face of difficulty, but that grows stronger with each challenge, knowing that God is working all things for our good and His glory.

Finally, the ultimate lesson from the Bible's battlefields is that victory is found in surrender—surrendering our plans, our fears, and our lives to the will of God. The battles of Scripture often required a total reliance on God, a willingness to let go of human strategies and to trust fully in His divine plan. This is perhaps the most difficult lesson to learn, yet it is the most crucial. In our walk with Christ, we are called to surrender our own understanding, to lean not on our own wisdom, but to acknowledge Him in all our ways, trusting that He will direct our paths. This surrender is not a sign of weakness, but of strength, for it aligns us with the power and purposes of God, enabling us to achieve victories that we could never accomplish on our own. As we conclude this journey through the Bible's battlefields, may we take these lessons to heart, applying them to every area of our lives, and walking in the victory that God has already secured for us through Christ. The battles we face are real, but so is our God, and in Him, we find the strength, the wisdom, and the courage to overcome. Let us therefore go forth with confidence, knowing that the same God who led His people to victory in ancient times is leading us today, and that in Him, we are more than conquerors.

Don't miss out!

Visit the website below and you can sign up to receive emails whenever Joshua Rhoades publishes a new book. There's no charge and no obligation.

https://books2read.com/r/B-A-AJLBB-JRRUE

BOOKS 2 READ

Connecting independent readers to independent writers.

Did you love *The Bible's Battlefields- Timeless Lessons from Ancient Wars*? Then you should read *Consider The Ant - God's Tiny Preachers*[1] by Joshua Rhoades!

[2]

In the vast and intricate world of creation, God has embedded profound lessons within the smallest of creatures, urging us to look beyond the obvious and consider the wisdom of the ant. In "Consider The Ant - God's Tiny Preachers," we look into the remarkable world of ants, those tiny but powerful teachers, whose lives reflect spiritual truths that can profoundly impact our walk with God. Proverbs 6:6 beckons us to "Go to the ant, thou sluggard; consider her ways, and be wise:" a call to observe and emulate the diligence, unity, and perseverance exemplified by these seemingly insignificant insects. Each type of ant, from the tireless worker to the vigilant soldier, reveals a facet of the Christian life, offering us insights into how we can better serve,

---

1. https://books2read.com/u/mB7LXR

2. https://books2read.com/u/mB7LXR

protect, and and lead. The worker ant, with its relentless dedication to gathering food and caring for the colony, mirrors the Christian's call to service, reminding us that no task in God's kingdom is too small or insignificant. The soldier ant, ever on guard to defend the colony, symbolizes the Christian's role in spiritual warfare, standing firm in the faith and safeguarding the truths of the gospel. Meanwhile, the queen ant, the heart of the colony, quietly embodies leadership and purpose, reflecting the importance of fulfilling our God-given roles with grace and dedication. Finally, the ant colony as a whole serves as a powerful metaphor for the local church, where each member, no matter how small, contributes to honoring the Lord, creating a thriving, harmonious body that mirrors the unity and effectiveness God desires for His church. As we explore these tiny preachers throughout this book, may we be inspired to embrace the lessons they offer, applying them to our lives so that we, too, may walk in wisdom, diligence, and unity, fulfilling our divine purpose in the grand design of God's kingdom.